No! I'm Watching Football!
Your Guide to a Successful Football Watching Relationship

Dedication

No! I'm Watching Football! is dedicated to my wife, Mary. She's a big football fan, just like me. When we were dating, I asked her to name the starting quarterbacks in pro football. She knew 29 of 31 and four back-ups! (This was before the Houston franchise was in the league) Not bad, 'huh? She accepted early on in our relationship that watching football was a priority for me and always will be.

About the Author

Tony Caputo is a New York Emmy Award Winning Television Journalist and self-proclaimed professional football junkie. He has worked in broadcasting for more than 20 years and continues to do so today as a reporter and anchor. He has loved watching pro football for more than 30 years and continues to do so every Sunday it's on!

Acknowledgements

A very special thank you to everyone listed here. Your support and time made No! I'm Watching Football! and www.noimwatchingfootball.com a reality.

Rick Sullivan: For his incredible cover art.

Taso Stefanidis: For creating the text and background on the front cover and uploading both the original front and back cover.

Kevin Smith: For updating the cover for the 2nd Edition.

Dennis Huntley (A Met Fan no less!): For uploading the PDF Files. Please visit: http://makingmsconnections.com to learn about a program Dennis runs to help provide computers to homebound sufferers of Multiple Sclerosis.

Joe Colon: For answering thousands of questions about PDF Files, QR codes and everything computer related. Contact Joe at: www.josephcolon.com

Larry Bailin
Owner of Single Throw Internet Marketing:
For creating noimwatchingfootball.com
Contact Larry at: www.singlethrow.com

Mary Caputo, Educational Consultant
Teach. Play. Inspire.
Check out Mary's web site at:
www.discoverytoyslink.com/marycap
Discovery Toys Inc. a Premier Educational Toy Company.

Talk football with **Tony Caputo at niwfootball@aol.com**

www.noimwatchingfootball.com

Introduction

Watching football games on Sunday is really very simple. You do not want to be bothered with working on the house...inside or out, any time after 1:00pm Eastern Time, which means if you want to shower before the game, yard work is finished by noon. (Please adjust for other time zones)

You want a significant other in your life who understands what these Sundays mean to you. It's not just "a game!" This is a part of your life; your happy life. When your team loses and you're dropping "F" bombs in front of the kids, you are indeed, happy! (That's not necessarily my style but if it works for you, you should have that right).

You want to pop open a beverage of choice, without someone saying, "How many is that?" You're home. You're not driving anywhere and you'll go to bed when ALL the games are over and you'll get up for work when the alarm goes off. You'll do this because you want to bust on your buddy who likes a different team...not to mention brag about your fantasy football team.

You DO NOT want to deal with the small percentage of couples in America who believe getting married on a Sunday in the fall is the right thing to do. It's wrong, plain and simple. Your significant other must know this about you. You're not going to a Sunday wedding in any month from September through early February. Not to mention, a Saturday wedding during the playoffs! It's just not happening.

One more note. This book is NOT just for men. There are many women who live for and love watching football. These and many other issues are covered in this guidebook. This is not simply a football fanatic attacking or bashing those who aren't. This is just a means of communication, so those who love watching the game, can do so, without interruption, frustration or interrogation. By the way, in some cases, you'll notice I don't mention specific names of people involved in my football life. Honestly, it's just easier that way and a lot less hassle. I have fantasy football to study anyway!

Enjoy!

1
Setting a Precedent

Do not forget at any time while reading this guide that your goal is to set a precedent with your significant other, family members and those in your immediate circle of life. They must know and understand that football comes first. Accomplish this and no more will you have to deal with the issues of life on a Sunday in the fall. YOU WILL COME FIRST. YOU WON'T BE BOTHERED AND YOU WILL SIT AND ENJOY ALL THE GAMES YOU WANT FROM THE COMFORT OF YOUR OWN HOME AND MAINTAIN A HAPPY, HEALTHY RELATIONSHIP WITH YOUR SIGNIFICANT OTHER, CHILDREN, FAMILY AND FRIENDS! IT CAN BE ACCOMPLISHED.

In real estate it's:
Location.
Location.
Location.

When it comes to watching pro football in the fall, it's:
Let this guide be your guide.
Let this guide be your guide.
Let this guide be your guide.

2
Defining Football

To fully understand what I'm trying to accomplish with this guidebook, we must make one thing clear. College Saturday's are NOT part of MY football experience. However, if college football is your game, my advice is to simply reverse the days (Saturday for Sunday) and apply to your life. For me, college football is good, only when your pro team stinks and you want to examine which "kid" will help your team in the future.

Instead of fighting with your significant other about Saturday afternoon, forget the college game. The championship system is a waste of time, and let's face it, MOST of the guys who play college football will never play a down in the pros. Instead, make your significant other happy. Go out shopping. Go to lunch and take a walk. Do whatever makes them happy in order to assure you will be able to watch as much football as you want on Sunday. This will also work to YOUR benefit. Avoiding football on Saturday is a good chance for you to relax. Chances are, all week long, while at work or working out and perhaps even with your significant other, you've been getting over last week's loss. Maybe getting pumped over your team's last second field goal and looking for another big win this week. It takes a lot out of a fan. Relax on Saturday...get away from the game....prepare for Sunday. That's the last I will speak on the college game. But again, if your passion is college football, I understand. Simply reverse the days and apply.

3
Becoming a Pro Football Fan

It all started in Fairless Hills, Pennsylvania. As a kid, growing up just outside of Philadelphia, I loved sports. My Uncle Bill, the biggest Phillies fan I have ever known, often took me and my brothers, Bob and John, to Phillies games. As a matter of fact, Veterans Stadium and its notorious reputation was the first place I ever smelled marijuana! (A story for another time, perhaps)

Now, although my brother John and many of my family members, including my mother, step father, his family and many others are all Eagles fans. I never liked the Eagles.

Here are the two reasons why.

When I was growing up in the '70's, the Eagles stunk. Because they weren't any good, they often did not sell out, which meant a TV blackout. At least that's how I remember it. Of course, not even being ten years old, it could have been because I was out playing. But, for whatever reason, every time I came in the house on a Sunday afternoon and the TV was on, I would see this stoic old man, with this very sharp suit and hat on, guiding his team from the sidelines. Then, I would see all these beautiful women dancing around. After that, #12 would throw some amazing pass and the Dallas Cowboys would win again! Tom Landry, the Dallas Cowboys cheerleaders and Roger Staubach. They did it. They made me a Cowboys fan. When Tex Schramm pulled some strings and somehow drafted Tony Dorsett, enough said. Even as a Penn State follower, everyone in Pennsylvania and around the country knew how great Dorsett was. I was a fan for life!

The second reason is because of my brother John's best friend, at the time. Growing up, he was a Cowboys fan (still is, I'm sure). He often wore this awesome hooded pullover that had a round Cowboys logo on it. I also seem to remember, either on the back of that hood or on another shirt was the # 44 with the name Newhouse; Fullback, Robert Newhouse. It was great stuff and very influential as a kid.

Not to mention those heartbreaking championship losses against the Steelers in the 70's. I also remember my Uncle Bill rubbing my head as if to say, don't worry about it, after the Steelers beat the Cowboys 35-31 in the second of their two classic big games.

As for loving the entire league as much as I do, I think a lot of it has to do with a tray I would often eat meals on as a kid. It was black and had all the football team's helmets. I would study that tray and those helmets all the time. Then, I would scrounge up quarters or ask my mom to get me the little plastic helmets out of the gumball machines at the store. I loved the logos on the helmets. Still do. As a matter of fact, I asked my wife to get me the shelf and plastic helmets you see in magazines. It now costs about $99.00! I really wish I still had that tray and those little helmets. But it sure was hard getting all the teams out of that gumball machine without getting doubles all the time.

Anyway, that's how my passion for Professional Football began.

4
The Shed

Let me give you an example of just what kind of pro football fan I am. After you read this, you'll want to do the same and yes, I recommend you do.

There was a time in my life when every Sunday, I would watch games sitting on a lawn mower or an old bench in my brother John's shed in his back yard. Yep...his shed.

It was the perfect scene for anyone who loves the game. We had a very old, very big, console television on the floor with his very big satellite dish wire pulled out of his house, running across the yard, through a hole we drilled in the shed wall, connecting us to the satellite football package! Viewing every game by satellite was relatively new and we took full advantage. But not only that, we also had two smaller TV's with rabbit ears to pick up the local games out of Philly. We also had a small refrigerator and plenty of ice and coolers and a working grill. No napkins were necessary.

Three TV's, food, beer and all the football you could want with the occasional fight over which game we were watching on the dish. We had me, the Cowboys fan, my brother, the Eagles fan, several other Eagles fans and a Denver Broncos fan.

One of the best parts of this set up was the fact that my brother's backyard was up against the Pennsylvania Turnpike. So noise was never an issue. There was plenty of distance between the shed and the road, so safety was never an issue either. He also had a wood fence separating the shed and his yard from the highway, which worked perfect for a bunch of guys drinking beer and grilling food all day.

Our bathroom was a small strip of land behind that fence, but facing the turnpike. Yep, as cars were whizzing by at 70-80 miles an hour, we were whizzing in the weeds! We would often wave and get an occasional horn. Good times.

Perhaps the best part was the fact that it was just guys, doing what guys like to do, without interruptions or issues about a dirty bathroom or carrying on in the basement. We were outside, like dogs, in good weather and in bad, loving every minute of it.

One of the best times I can remember was on a very cold day in, I believe November or could have been early December. Remember the game when Barry Switzer was the Cowboys head coach and they were in Philly and he ran Emmitt Smith on two consecutive fourth and inches plays and the Eagles stopped them both times? They ran the play the first time, didn't make it, but there was a penalty. So Switzer, getting the fourth down over, attempted to go for it again and ran the same exact play with Emmitt Smith and he was stopped stone cold again on that frozen Veterans Stadium turf.

We were all in the shed that day. I was shivering, not only from the weather, but I also had a fever! But that was a game I was not going to miss. There were three Eagles fans in the shed including my brother and the Bronco's fan, not to mention my brother's son, who, at the time was a 49ers fan. (He has since become an Eagles fan, influence from Dad I guess) Anyway, back in The Shed, the beer was flowing. When the Eagles stopped them twice and went on to win the game, the Philly fans were going crazy. As they were celebrating, the Bronco's fan said, "I'm changing the channel, I want to watch the Broncos game on the dish." But this was an Eagles day, and those three wanted no part of watching their victorious post game on a small TV with rabbit ears!

13

So they jumped the Broncos fan. Not an all-out, old west, type of bar fight. There weren't any punches thrown, but it was a brawl nonetheless. The Broncos fan definitely held his own. I'm sure he didn't drink nearly as much that day. The battle raged in The Shed and outside The Shed, in the snow and on the wet ground. My nephew who was around 12 at the time, and I, just cowered in the corner. Me, because of my fever (I'll use that as my excuse!)

In the end, the small window in the shed was broken, the Eagles fans missed their post-game coverage and the dish was eventually changed to watch the Broncos game. It was quite a memorable day in The Shed. (Actually known as, "Shed Two." Again, a story for another day) I got the last laugh, however. The Cowboys beat the Steelers in the big game that same year.

5
Weddings

Weddings are a wonderful time. Family, friends and way too much money spent on what's supposed to be the single greatest day in a couple's life. That's great. Except for the guy or two who sneaks a small radio in with them and pops in an earpiece that is running up through his suit coat in order to listen to his team during the reception.

Honestly, I had a hard enough time going to a wedding during the pro basketball playoffs a few years back. So I can tell you, there is NO WAY I'm going to any wedding during a football Sunday. My wife knows to tell relatives or anyone else that her husband will not be attending a wedding, birthday, Bar/Bat Mitzvah, funeral or anything else when the game is on!

Here's a story that really bugs me every time it crosses my mind. The Steelers vs. Jets, 2004 Playoffs. A buddy of mine who lives in Staten Island, New York is one of the biggest STEELERS fans I know. Yes, you would think he would be a Jets or Giants fan, but that's the beauty of pro football. It's cool to like a team from anywhere in the country and makes for great arguments! Anyway, he met this girl and he really liked her. But after watching a rookie quarterback, Ben Roethlisberger, take over his team and guide them to an incredible regular season, he had to GO TO A WEDDING instead of being able to watch the game! HAD TO GO TO A WEDDING!

Now, I give him credit. I would have left her almost immediately. He went to the wedding, but as I touched on earlier, he took a small radio with him so he could hear what was going on. But it shouldn't have to be that way. Why does he have to respect her wishes to go to a wedding? Why can't she respect HIS wishes to watch a team that he has loved for years? He hardly even knew the people who were getting married.

You see, I set a precedent early in my relationship with my wife. When we were dating, her relatives threw a birthday party for a wonderful young man who is now my nephew. The party started around 3pm. Instead of going to the home where the party was, I stayed, by myself at my wife's grandparent's house in Nutley, New Jersey, watching the Cowboys vs. 49ers game. It turned out to be the game where Terrell Owens ran to mid-field and spiked the ball on the Cowboys famous star. The Niners won. I was pissed, but the beauty of it was, when I arrived at the party a mile or so away, nobody was mad. They didn't fully understand, but nobody was mad. When my wife tells those relatives that I will not be making an event because of football, they understand. Some think it's a bit lame, but that's OK with me. As long as they let me be and don't hold a grudge, it has all worked out.

Oh, by the way, the Steelers beat the Jets in that game. My buddy watched the HIGHLIGHTS later that night. The highlights, pathetic and it didn't have to be that way. Especially considering that couple is no longer together! So, in the end, he missed that awesome game for nothing! Unless, of course, he got some action that night...then...maybe....MAYBE....it was worth it. Maybe.

I SAY, WATCH THE GAME AND GET SOME ACTION!

Here's how. Set the precedent early in your relationship, as I did. Don't give in as you're dating....that will only continue into the marriage, if it goes that far. You are preparing for your future in which you are happy, watching football. Stick to your guns. If it doesn't work out because of your decisions now, trust me, it will only work to your football watching benefit in the future when you're with your next significant other and you will be a much happier, responsible, football watching adult! You have to trust me and stick to this plan or you will suffer greatly, later in life.

Without question, the best groomsman gifts I've ever seen at any wedding were given by an old friend of mine, Tom McCarthy. This is the same Tom McCarthy who is also the Play-By-Play voice for the Philadelphia Phillies.

The irony here is that I got into the business of broadcasting to either be the next Howard Stern or the next Harry Kalas.

OK, there will never be another Howard Stern or Harry Kalas. But if I had listened to Tom many years ago, perhaps I could have been the next Tom McCarthy!

Hear me out.

Tom and I worked together at WZBN-TV in Mercer County, New Jersey long, long ago. At the time, county officials were doing their best to bring a minor league baseball team to Trenton. Today, that team is the New York Yankees Double A affiliate, the Trenton Thunder.

Tom pulled me aside one day and said, "Tony, why don't you and I put in for the announcing jobs for this new team. I'm sure we'll get them." As I recall, I believe I said I was enjoying news and since I was anchoring the show, I felt that's where I belonged. I also didn't love the idea of working nights and weekends for much of the year and the thought of having to announce baseball games when there was pro football being played was way too much for me to comprehend!! Announcing baseball when football was on? C'mon now.

So I declined.

Tom moved forward and got that Thunder announcing job (at the time, Trenton was the Double A affiliate of the

Detroit Tigers) and has since worked for the New York Mets as well as the Phillies.

Well done old friend. Well done.

And I enjoy listening to Tom every Phillies game I watch.

Now it was around that same time, Tom got married. At the wedding, I noticed something that really caught my eye! His groomsmen were carrying around football jerseys! Tom gave each of his groomsman a football jersey of their favorite team!!!! Damn Tom. You couldn't have asked me to be in the wedding party?
The best groomsman gifts I've ever seen.

Well done old friend. Well done.

6
Building The Reputation
YOU Want

By setting a precedent with not only your significant other, but also family members, in time, you will build a reputation. It may not be pretty all the time, but it will get you what we are working for and that is, your time for watching pro football. I can't tell you how many times family members of mine have given me sarcastic or sly comments like, "Well, Tony won't be there, he'll have to watch football." I have always just smiled and moved on or at times have said, "That's right," with a friendly, I don't give a s_ _ t what you think smile.

A perfect example for building a reputation took place around Thanksgiving, 2006. For the third straight year, my wife's cousin and her husband invited us to their home for Thanksgiving. I love their home. All my life, I have looked at houses that I have loved and often referred to them as, great Thanksgiving houses. You know the type of home I'm talking about. It just has a look that seems to say, "hey, come on in, I'll make you comfortable and warm and you'll feel welcome the entire time you're here. And oh, by the way, you'll feed your face with some of the best food you've ever eaten and when you're finished, I won't ask you to help clean-up, you just go and relax and watch some football"! That is what this home is like and that is exactly the treatment I receive when I go there.

When I arrived on that rainy and cold yet wonderful Thursday, November 23, 2006, I said with a smile, "look, I've been here the past two years and the Cowboys have lost. (Dolphins and Broncos) If they lose again this year, I'm not coming back!" They are Giant fans and probably couldn't give a crap if I came back or not! That being said, we all have a great time together, drinking beer, an incredible meal and football. By the way, the Cowboys smoked Tampa Bay and QB Tony Romo tied Troy Aikman's team record by throwing five touchdown passes. You remember the game; Terrell Owens caught one of those passes, ran through the end zone and dropped the ball into the big Salvation Army bucket next to the stands. Great stuff for a Cowboys fan, but let's get back to why building a reputation paid off.

As Thursday approached, I was talking to my wife on the phone while I was at work. She tells me she just spoke with her cousin and everything is ready to go and they look forward to spending the afternoon with us. Then she tells my wife, "Tell Tony he can sit at the head of the table, so he has a perfect view of the Cowboys game, if we're not finished eating by kickoff!"

THAT'S WHAT I'M TALKIN' ABOUT!

Here she is getting ready to prepare this awesome Thanksgiving meal with all the trimmings. She and her husband are doing creative things like putting two carrots and celery sticks under the turkey so its juice drips into the pan while it's in the oven, yet they're both thinking of the well-being of the guy who MUST watch the Cowboys play on Thanksgiving. Turkey, stuffing, gravy and five touchdown passes from Tony Romo on a large screen TV somewhere in the great state of New Jersey.

I'd say it was a Thanksgiving to remember and a perfect way for you to remember that building a reputation, good or bad, will pay off for you and your enjoyment of watching the game we love.

7
Giving In

OK. It's time.

I will admit there has been a time or two when I have given into the responsibilities of life and marriage and have taken care of the kids on a football Sunday. Hard to believe, but it is true.

Case in point: November 5, 2006.

My wife is a Discovery Toys Consultant. In other words, she sells toys. But not just any toys, high end, educational toys that we are raising our children on. They are an excellent product and offer a lifetime guarantee. (Notice this very special endorsement by her loving and devoted husband)

Anyway, on this particular Sunday, she was part of a show in Nutley, New Jersey and yes, I gave up this one Sunday for her, even though the Cowboys were taking on the Redskins; one of the greatest rivalries in sports.

Those of you familiar with the game know how it ended. An agonizing defeat for Cowboys fans all over the country and the world. Hollywood could not have scripted a more difficult ending for the losing team. Early in the game with the Redskins leading 5-0 after a field goal and a safety, the Cowboys scored their first touchdown. For some reason, soon to be Hall of Fame head coach Bill Parcells thought it was the right move going for the two point conversion. The Cowboys did not convert and led 6-5. This would come back to haunt them. Later, in the third quarter and the Cowboys up by a touchdown, Terrell Owens dropped a sure touchdown pass after Romo hit him on the hands, in stride...a perfectly thrown bomb. But again, Owens dropped the ball. Later, the Redskins tied the game at 19 with a touchdown pass of their own.

So it came down to this.

About 35 seconds left in the game, still tied at 19 and the Redskins attempted a 49 yard field goal...which went wide right! Ok, I thought as a Cowboys fan, let's go to overtime or even better, move downfield with the time we have left and kick a field goal to win this baby!

And that's what the Cowboys did. Only the field goal by the Cowboys was blocked and the Redskins ran it back inside Cowboys territory with no time left on the clock. On to overtime, right? Oh, did I mention the 15 yard face mask penalty against the Cowboys? Yep. Redskins get one free play, again, with no time on the clock, kicked a field goal and won the game.

It was one of the most difficult losses I ever had to accept as a sports fan. And while all this was happening, I'm feeding my daughters, Patricia and Sophia, who were three years old and 19 months respectively, yogurt.

They cheer when I cheer. They scream when I scream. In this case, we all just got quiet once the game was over....they just followed my lead, staring at the screen asking, "What just happened here?"

It was a tough loss. A tough day, but a successful sacrifice for family life!

So, in a sense, a victory.

8
How Giving In Can Pay Off

Let's move forward to September, 2007.

While living in New Jersey, the home we had purchased three years before had a major issue. Because my work hours had me getting up at 2:00 AM, every weekday morning, I usually slept downstairs, alone in our bi-level home. My wife and daughters would sleep upstairs. We did this so I could actually get some sleep while the kids were busy playing upstairs. Anyway, while laying there one night, and it was very quiet, I heard what sounded to me like someone pouring water out of a gallon jug, UNDER MY HOUSE. The house is built on a slab... no basement... no crawl space. It had rained for several days before, so I thought little of it and hoped for the best. Until the water bill arrived. It was five times higher than the previous year! To make a long story short, our water line was leaking, under my house and I was paying for two gallons of water every minute which was doing nothing more than supplying H2O to the worms. I called the plumber. Plumber fixed the issue.... for $5300.00. Yeah. Five thousand, three hundred dollars!

So what can all of this have to do with successfully watching Sunday football you ask?

Here you go.

I say to my wife, "we need to cut corners AND make more money in order to make ends meet." First thing I could think of to cut back is to take away something that I Do, you know, to set an example of the sacrifices we must now make to make ends meet and pay off this ever climbing credit card debt. I mean, it's not like we had five grand lying around to give to the plumber!
So I say, "I'll give up the satellite football package." And as I said it, I thought, there goes my Guide Book to

Successfully Watching Pro Football." I mean, any guy who has to give up the football package, can't write a book like this, can he? No he can't!

So week one rolls around and the Cowboys open the season on Sunday Night national television. I also happen to live in a part of New Jersey where the local cable company gives you both New York and Philadelphia stations. That means you can get more NFL game choices during the year.

So week one, without the football package, I did OK. I watched the Eagles vs. Packers at 1pm as well as the Jets vs. Patriots. (Used two TV's...just like the 'ol Shed days!) At 4pm I watched a hard hitting Bears vs. Chargers game. Then, I watched Cowboys vs. Giants Sunday night. No problems in week one.

But week two was another issue.

The Cowboys were playing in Miami at 4pm and for some reason, both New York and Philadelphia TV execs did not think that game was worthy to be shown in either market. Knowing this long before Sunday, I panicked and said to my wife, "Hey, there is no way I'm not watching the game this Sunday. We need to get the package!" Now look, I love watching Sunday football and if you've read this far you know that by now. But I'm the first to admit, the satellite football package is WAY too expensive. But when you're addicted, like me, you must have what you must have.

Now keep in mind our earlier chapter appropriately named, "Giving In," as I tell you the rest of the story. After I said to my wife, "We need to get the package!" She didn't argue with me. She also realized it's possible, living where we live, that we could be paying hundreds of dollars for ONE game, considering I might be able to see every other Cowboys game on one of the stations out of New York or Philly for the remainder of the season.

Instead, she picked up the phone, called that Sunday morning and by kickoff, there I was watching the Cowboys at Dolphins.

Nice!

Oh, did I mention that my wife was working again on this particular Sunday and again, just like in the "Giving In" chapter, I was watching the kids! But the beauty of life is that kids keep getting older which meant they were a little more independent and easier on Daddy. I also took them outside to run around and play from 11am to 1pm AND invited my friend John down to 'keep them company as well'.

It's all little tricks of the trade to get your significant other on board as well as entertain the kids and hang out with a friend, while getting exactly what you want.

I'll call it "the tri-fecta"

1) Happy Wife.
2) Kids are entertained.
3) Buddy over the house watching football.

No, no, no, don't thank me. It's information that I've wanted to share with you for a long, long time.

Before we leave this chapter, I should also say that the touchdown channel, as I like to call it, which is available these days through the cable company, is also a great option. Again, the satellite football package is amazing allowing you to watch every game in its entirety. But it's not affordable. If you are like me, you pretty much watch football alone at home. So I have adjusted to the touchdown channel and take advantage of the local New York and Philly channels. I still see most if not all Cowboys games throughout the season.

One more note. The Internet is now providing games as well, even though it may not be legal here in the United States. Although league officials may not like this, I can't imagine there is anything they can do to stop games from being found on the Internet. So watching games on-line allows access to see every game you want and not spend a month's salary to do so, again keeping your significant other happy!

9
How to Survive Football Season

How to survive football season was not my idea for a chapter. However, as I was eating a bowl of cereal one Saturday morning, talking with my kids and my wife, I came across this segment in a parenting magazine. It was just a small portion of the page but was listed, "Smart Solutions, Reality Check. How To Survive Football Season." I thought this ought to be good, considering it was in a parenting magazine and showed a guy on the couch with a football actually looking happy. Perfect, I thought, a husband looking happy...so lets write an article about how we can ensure he's not that happy all the time!

In bold, you will read what was written in the magazine first, and then I'll give you my response.

1) Make Him Choose: Decide (together!) that a dad with little kids can no longer watch college and pro but must limit himself to one game per day.

I agree with half of this. I made it clear from the start of this book that Saturday is the day to take care of the family. So you can free up your Sunday for ALL DAY SUNDAY FOOTBALL. But what's this about one game? Are you kidding me? That is just crazy spouse talk. I suggest you remind your significant other that you are home, with the family, enjoying something you love. You're not at a bar; you're not a great distance from the family in any way. Want me to be with the kids? No problem. Have them watch the games with me. How do you accomplish that you ask? I recommend a game I've been playing for years with my children called, "fumbles." Get a football and crawl around with them constantly hitting the ball and yelling, "Fumble!" Then once you or your kid gets it, make sure it comes loose again and play some more. Sure it makes it hard to change the channel while watching the football package, but trust me, you'll get good at it and everyone will be happy. Plus, kids have a short attention span. They'll be back playing in their rooms or watching their own shows in no time. Everyone is happy in the end when you put this approach to use. You'll even start to look forward to playing "fumbles" more often.

2) Mute the Commercials: Yeah, some of them are fun, but lots for beer, erectile dysfunction pills, horror movies-may be less than appropriate for kids.

No problem here. The satellite football package or touchdown channel always allows me to not just mute the commercials, but not watch them. There's always a game on...always. By the way, I don't like horror movies. (after seeing Blair Witch Project, I couldn't sleep for a week) Plus the fact that I already have kids, means that maybe it's better if I have an issue or two with erectile dysfunction!

3) Divvy up Child Chasing: If you're both fans, you do vigilance and diapers first quarter; he does it during the second and so on. That way, you both can enjoy the game.

I'm OK with this to a certain extent. Look, I'll admit, I have changed my kids' diapers during games. But let's just take it easy with the sharing of child chasing. To what extent are we talking about here? If my daughter says she wants me to color with her during Sunday football, she knows my response, "No, football." My wife knows that is my response as well. Why do they know this?...Setting a precedent. Which takes us all the way back to the first few sentences in this wonderful guide you're now planning to carry in your back pocket for the rest of your football watching life! Again, I don't mind helping with the kids, but this 50/50 thing isn't always going to fly. Just like in other aspects of life. You know, like cleaning gutters or painting or earning a living. It's not always a 50/50 deal. Look, if you and your spouse both enjoy watching football, life doesn't get any better and you'll work it out. Perhaps, setting up diapers and wipes and such BEFORE the games begin. Be prepared at all times. But if you ask me, more responsibility with the kids goes to the person who doesn't think the game is as important. Whether it's your team or a fantasy football thing or you have some money riding on it, that's what should ultimately make the decision. Not, "for better or worse, for richer or poorer, 'til death do us part, hey, it's your quarter to change the diaper!" No way. Find your own happy medium.

4) Leave Him Alone: (with your children, that is) Go for coffee, hit the mall, head to the gym and let Mr. Sofa-pants deal with the kids. They'll be fine.

What a bunch of ridiculous crap this is. First of all, what's with the "him?" As you can see, I have worked very hard to make sure I refer to the other person in your life as your spouse, not making this a him/her situation. This parenting magazine just assumed only the man wants to watch a lot of pro football...not always the case today my friends. Second, why on earth would I say it's ok for my wife to go out and do something fun during football season? There are six other days during the week and seven days in the other six months of the year she can do that. Are you telling me my spouse can't respect my wishes enough NOT to go out when there is football on? And if so, are you telling me she wouldn't be willing to take the kids knowing I'm doing nothing wrong and what I love to do and look forward to doing more than anything on earth? I mean, she knows I love watching every single minute of as many games as I can! She's knows I'm home and not out looking for another woman or wasting our money at a bar or on a golf course! C'mon now. How about a little respect for the one who says, "I'll be home honey, you know that. I just really want to watch football, all day long."

Look, several of the points made in the magazine I can live with. But I really just read this article as an "in your face" kind of dig at men. That's just not right. I'll give you Saturdays (in my world anyway, since I'm not a major college football fan) but don't tell me that its wrong for me to watch more than four hours of football a week and oh, I should change diapers and chase the kids during two of the four quarters I've been waiting all week for! That crap just really pisses me off and that's basically why I'm writing this book.

Here's something else you may have seen that also upsets me. There's a fast food commercial in which a husband and wife are eating breakfast and she says something like, "My sister says her new boyfriend believes Sunday's are for just watching football, you believe that?" Hearing this, he starts to panic and while thinking to himself about how to respond, he pictures his wife throwing him out of the house for not saying what she considers to be the correct response.

Are you kidding me?

Anyway, he eventually comes up with this 'genius' response.

"He's a jerk."

The wife smiles. He pats himself on the back and with true marital bliss, they go on to finish their breakfast.

Are you kidding me?

My response would have been, "Oh yeah, we need to meet this guy! He sounds like a keeper for your sister!" And with true marital bliss we would have gone on to finish our breakfast.

Remember, honesty is the best policy!

10
My Pro Football Days

I never played a down in the pro's.

I never even put on a uniform.

But I smelled them. Uniforms I mean. And that wasn't always pleasant; Even if they were worn by stars like Montana, Irvin and Walker.

In my early years of broadcasting, I worked at WPHL-TV 17 in Philadelphia as a Master Control Summer Relief Technician. Master Control in television is where someone makes sure everything that goes on-air does so properly and at the right time. Summer Relief Technician means I only worked during the summer months when the union employees went on vacation. So for a little more than three months a year I would find myself working wonderful shifts like 7:00 PM - 4:00 AM, loading commercials into a big, bulky machine that often jammed. I would also load the big reel-to-reel movies and when it would all go smoothly, it made for a long, but quiet night. When something went wrong, it made for a long, difficult night. But I was about 21-22 years old and the union was paying me pretty good money for someone who never went to college, so I didn't complain. What I didn't realize at the time was how it would lead to some on-field experience at Philadelphia's Veterans Stadium.

The more I worked at Channel 17, the better I got to know everyone involved. Including Billy Egbert, who, as I recall, was the union President. I would ask Billy at the end of each summer if he could swing some more work for me during the fall/winter months. Out of the blue he called me. He lined up some work with CBS Sports whenever the Eagles played a home game. I think he also asked me if I knew anything about football and if I liked the game. Ha! I went through the roof! I asked him what I would do there and he said, "You'll pull cable for the on-field, hand held camera man. So you'll be on the field, next to the players and the cheerleaders for most of the game. CBS will feed you before and after the game and someone will always be telling you what you need to do."

I was in my early 20's. Not a care in the world. And I was being paid to run around the Astroturf at Veterans Stadium to watch pro football, stand next to beautiful cheerleaders and meet, or at least be near, some of the biggest stars to ever play the game!

They included...

Terry Bradshaw

I'd be lying if I said I could remember the exact game I had the chance to chat with Terry Bradshaw. I do recall being on the field when he interviewed Joe Montana (that story coming up!) but I would assume Terry was in the booth for many games I worked since the Buddy Ryan led Eagles were a very good team back then. At this point in his broadcasting career, Bradshaw was the color commentator for CBS and not yet in studio.

As I recall, I not only worked all day Sunday for CBS, but I also had an overnight radio shift as a disc jockey at WBCB-AM 1490 in Bucks County, Pennsylvania at that time as well. That was a regular, Saturday night into Sunday Morning shift, midnight to 6:00 AM. So when the Eagles played a home game I would wind up working close to 24 straight hours. But again, I was young, had the energy and needed money to help pay the rent! (I was sharing an apartment at the time with Tom, the Raiders fan from the "Beer Bet" chapter and it would drive him crazy that I would make my share of the rent by working a 24 hour period and sit around the rest of the week! But Tom did help me out, picking up my share of the rent those weeks when the Eagles were on the road. Thanks again Tom!

Anyway, the night before the game as I'm working my DJ job, I was looking through a Billboard Top 100 book. This was long before you could use the Internet to pass the time. So as I'm looking through I noticed a Terry Bradshaw song called, "I'm So Lonesome I Could Cry." I was shocked to see Terry made the Top 100 in the Pop Song category! I thought, if I get a chance to see him at Veterans Stadium I'm going to ask him if he knew his song was on the Pop chart.

Fast forward a few hours, about 8:00 AM that Sunday morning. I was sitting in the early morning production meeting with CBS Sports. Very exciting! (I've since learned that most meetings, of any kind, are dramatically boring) As I'm sitting there minding my own business, listening to the seasoned production pro's at CBS crack jokes and chew the fat, who walks in but Terry Bradshaw.

As he walked to the front of the room I yelled out, "Terry!" He looked over and with that happy go lucky smile of his, he said. "How are ya?" I told him I worked as a disc jockey as well and noticed one of his songs in the Billboard Top 100 book. I said, "Can you tell me how high on the chart your song got?" With a big smile he yelled out, "Number 1!" Everyone, including me laughed and the whole room turned to look at me, waiting for my answer. I said, "Nope, number 91." He said, "Wait a minute, that was on the Pop Charts, but on the Country Charts my song went all the way to Number 1!"

A good laugh was had by all.

Joe Montana

Only two pro quarterbacks in history can say they've won four Super Bowls. (At least as I'm writing this)

I just talked about Terry Bradshaw. The other is Joe Montana. I've been fortunate enough to be within a few feet of both of them. When I was with Montana, Terry Bradshaw was there as well, on the field at Veterans Stadium. This game I remember clearly. September of 1989.

Buddy Ryan's Eagles were dominating the 49ers. Everyone in Philly was talking Super Bowl with Randall Cunningham at quarterback, Reggie White and Jerome Brown leading Buddy's vaunted "46" Defense that dominated when he was defensive coordinator for the 1985 Chicago Bears. Beating the 49ers would lift the Eagles to 3-0 start and give the team and the city some serious bragging rights early on.

The Eagles led 12-10 at the half and had a 21-10 lead early in the 4th quarter. And even after Montana cut that lead to 21-17, the Eagles scored again to up their advantage to 28-17.

But this was Joe Montana they were playing.

The Notre Dame grad proceeded to throw three more 4th quarter touchdowns to show the nation that a "46" defense was no match for number 16.

Final Score: 49ers 38 - Eagles 28

As the frustrated Eagles faithful were filing out of the Vet, I stayed on the field with the cameraman, waiting for the post-game interview. Terry Bradshaw came down from the booth and was waiting for Joe Montana. And so did some of the loudest, toughest, most rude Eagles fans you'd ever want to hear!

Growing up in Philly as a Phillies and 76ers fan, I was used to this. Growing up a Cowboys fan, I was used to this being directed at me! So I wasn't surprised. I thought it was kind of funny. They were even yelling stuff at

Terry...you know, the guy who won four championships on the other side of the state!

Montana came back out of the locker room and jogged across the field in his uniform pants but only had a t-shirt with no pads. I'm not a large man by any stretch, but even I couldn't believe how skinny Joe Montana was. I saw this guy take beatings on the field and I couldn't comprehend how he was not only still standing, but winning and winning often!

As we're standing there waiting for the commercials to end and the interview to begin, Eagles fans were relentless. Some were yelling, "You suck Montana" or "We'll see you in the playoffs and kick your ass Montana". I'm being kind here. There was much worse being yelled out, but you get the idea.

Then I watched as the one and only Joe Montana did something I would never think he would do. He looked up at the crowd, smiled and then....grabbed his balls as if to say, "Here, this is for you!"

I cracked up laughing and loved every second of it.

Eagles' fans were furious, shouting back, "You really suck Montana...can't wait until Reggie and Jerome rip your F'in head off in the playoffs! Classic Philly Eagles fans taking on arguably the greatest quarterback of all time.

Phil Simms

When Phil Simms first started playing QB for the Giants, I loved to take verbal shots at him. It just seemed too easy.

That blond hair and what appeared to be a frail looking body. On the football field with huge lineman running around, most QB's back then looked small compared to the rest of the players.

As the Cowboys-Giants would play I would yell things like, "Knock that sissy down" or "Get that little girl!" From the safety of my couch, I could yell and scream anything I wanted. As a crazed football fan, I liked to believe he and any other player could hear me yell and scream!

Once again, while working at Veterans Stadium I was standing in the back of the elevator, waiting to make my way upstairs for another CBS production meeting. All of a sudden, a very large, very intimidating man with blond hair made his way on to the elevator as well.

Yep. It was Phil Simms. As he stood next to me, I was quiet. Waiting for him to look down on me and say, 'Hey, I could hear every word you said and every name you called me from that couch of yours...have anything to say now?!?!?!' My answer would have been no, of course. But I swear, while standing there, he could hear my thoughts! Which, at that time were, boy, I sure am tough sitting on the couch...all 5' 8" - 165 pounds of me...go ahead tough guy, call him some of those names now!

The elevator stopped. Simms walked off. I never even said hello to the man. But I learned a valuable lesson.

Be careful who you mouth off to. You never know when you may share an elevator with them.

Herschel Walker

I was fortunate to meet Herschel Walker a couple of times. Each time was about as pleasant an experience as you could imagine. Truly, one of the nicest athletes I've ever met. So much so, that he thanked me on the field at Veterans Stadium when he was a member of the Minnesota Vikings!

It was just after the famous trade between the Vikings and Cowboys. The Cowboys were a very bad team. Jerry

Jones and Jimmy Johnson had just taken over and Herschel Walker was one of the few good players they had.

Minnesota thought it was on the verge of a Super Bowl Championship and felt it needed one top notch player to get it done. Herschel Walker was supposed to be that player. After trading about a dozen players and what seemed to be 50 draft picks, the Vikings had their man and the Cowboys had their plan.

The rest is history.

But on the field at Veterans Stadium, as Herschel was stretching, I walked right past him. I quickly said, "Thanks for the great times in Dallas Herschel. I'm a Cowboys fan and you were always fun to watch." He said, "Thank you man, I really appreciate that."

I'll never forget it. It was genuine and from the heart.

I also met him years later when I was hosting a radio show in Bucks County, Pennsylvania and he was a member of the Eagles; again, polite and professional.

I think he's still, if not one of the few players in history to have a run, a catch and a kick return for a touchdown of more than 90 yards in his career. He put up some great numbers as a pro. I'm sure he made many friends along the way as well.

Keith Millard

For a short time Keith Millard was one of the best defensive linemen in football. He seemed to play at a thousand percent on every down.

Minnesota Vikings fans loved him. I met Millard the same day I met Herschel Walker, on the field at Veterans Stadium. But this experience was quite different.

Millard was out early, stretching right around mid-field on that terrible Astroturf at the Vet. If you're not familiar with just how bad the turf was at the Vet, Google it. You'll read some very interesting stories, trust me.

Anyway, as Millard was stretching I followed my cameraman, a guy named Kenny Woo, out to greet Millard. Kenny put the video camera on the field to get some b-roll (as it's called in the business) of Millard doing his thing. But Millard didn't like it. From about five yards away, Keith looked at Kenny and gently said, "Get that camera out of my face!" Kenny didn't budge. I was about five yards behind Kenny shaking in my sneakers! It seemed to be so quiet at that point, you could hear an Eagles fan in the 700 Level (upper deck) yelling something nasty.

After a few more seconds passed Millard stopped stretching, reached to put his hand on the front of the camera (which was now in Kenny's arms), pushed as hard as he could and screamed, "I TOLD YOU TO GET THAT F'KIN CAMERA OUT OF MY FACE!"

Kenny rolled about five yards with the camera flying just behind him. I stood there, not having any idea what to do!

Kenny picked himself up, picked up his camera, looked at the scared guy working with him and said, "Let's go."

Keith Millard. It was nice to meet you.

Reggie White

Let's see. I told you that I worked as a disc jockey, in master control, pulled cable for a CBS Sports cameraman and my current position as a television reporter.

Did I mention I was also a producer for a sports talk radio station? 610-WIP in Philadelphia. This job was only for a short time, but I did get to meet and work with some big local and national names.

One of the local stars was Howard Eskin, who has been a mainstay in Philly sports for years. Howard comes across as a tough dude and will go toe-to-toe with anyone, but he was always professional with me. (I'm certain he wouldn't even remember working with me.)

One night, I was helping to produce a show at a sports bar in Center City Philadelphia and the guest was none other than the "Minister of Defense!"

The late, great Reggie White.

As I met Reggie, I noticed his entire family was with him. There was his wife and children, including a very young son. Somehow, playing with Reggie's son became my immediate responsibility.

Hey, the kid was cute and we were having fun. He had a ball and we were throwing it back and forth.

Then it hit me. This is Reggie White's kid. If he gets hurt jumping up and down on what was a small stage at this sports bar, everyone is going to look to me for an explanation. The host of the show. The other producer. Eventually, my boss and most important, THE "Minister of Defense" himself!

It was then I walked the little guy over to his mom and said, "Here you go." Safe and sound. The kid and me!

Jason Garrett

I met Jason Garrett following a Cowboys win over the Jets on a Saturday afternoon at the old Giants Stadium in East Rutherford, New Jersey back in the early 90's.

I was covering the game for one reason. To interview Garrett who, at the time, was the Cowboys third string QB.

I worked for WZBN-TV 25 in Hamilton, New Jersey. Hamilton is located just next to the state capital, Trenton. It's also located in Mercer County. WZBN is a low-power station which covers anything and everything about Mercer County.

Knowing Princeton and Princeton University are located in Mercer County and knowing Jason Garrett is a graduate of Princeton University, I convinced the owners of the station to do a story on him and how he was persevering following his demotion back to third string. The Cowboys acquired former Cleveland Browns quarterback Bernie Kosar to back up Troy Aikman.

My boss and camerman, Greg Zanoni and I met Jason in the locker room following the game. Knowing he was just demoted to third string and really never played all that much backing up Troy Aikman, he was probably a bit surprised anyone wanted to talk to him. Then again, being back in New Jersey, where he went to college, maybe he wasn't so shocked. Either way, it was a great conversation with a great guy. (Would love to have the chance again today!) He took everything in stride. He talked about how it was his responsibility to keep working hard and to be ready when and if his time came. Although I could sense some disappointment in the acquisition of Kosar, Garrett never flinched. A true professional.

I also threw a microphone in Emmitt Smith's face while he was at his locker. Emmitt was a typical after the game interview with plenty of media. As I recall, I snuck in a late question to him about Jason Garrett. He said something quick like, "Jason's a great teammate."

Jerry Jones

I met Jerry on the same day I met Garrett and Michael Irvin (his story coming up).

Members of the media were standing outside the locker room area following the game, waiting to get access inside. I was young and really didn't fit in that well. So I simply waited along with Greg for any indication the media can go inside.

As we were standing there, who walks toward all of us but Jerry Jones.

Now Jerry had certainly made plenty of waves and got a lot of attention after buying the Cowboys. He fired Tom Landry; hired Jimmy Johnson and made America's Team a powerhouse again.

I quickly realized if I was to talk with Jerry Jones, it would have to be right now.

I stopped him as he was walking by, introduced myself and told him I was there to interview Jason Garrett. He looked at me, smiled and said he would be happy to talk about Jason.

I was on Cloud Nine.

Jerry went on to tell me how impressed he was with Jason's ability to not only continue to be the back-up QB on a team with a superstar at the position, but how professionally he was handling the Bernie Kosar signing.

He was more than happy to take a moment and talk about a guy that it appeared everyone on the team was truly fond of.

Michael Irvin

I saved this one for last for a reason. It's my favorite.

I enjoy telling my Michael Irvin story more than any other because it taught me, at an early age, how to do my job as a television reporter.

Michael Irvin was one of the last Cowboys to leave the locker room that same night I interviewed Jason Garrett and Jerry Jones.

I saw him standing there, in the distance, by himself. How could I not see him? He was wearing a Superman shaped medallion on his necklace. It appeared to be filled with diamonds.

As I approached him, he gave me a look as if to say, kid, if you talk to me, I may kill you. And why not? It was late. The game had ended well over an hour ago and most of his teammates were waiting on the bus to get to the airport and back home to Dallas.

Although I was seriously intimidated, I pressed on. As I was introducing myself, his look never changed. But then, I said what appeared to be the magic words. Jason Garrett.

When I told him I wanted to talk to him about Jason Garrett his face lit up. His smile was ear to ear. He said, "Jason, that's my boy! What do you want to know?"

We talked for what seemed like a half hour. He answered every question I had and went on to say that he and

Jason often worked together after practice, running routes and so on.

He loved Jason Garrett.

Michael taught me something I will always remember. You truly can't judge a book by its cover.

As I continue to work as a television reporter, I've experienced this many times, both in positive and negative situations.   Sometimes, it appears as if someone doesn't want to be interviewed and they do. Sometimes, they look approachable and tell me to get lost.

Thanks to Michael Irvin, I never stop trying. No matter how they look at me.

11
The Beer Bet

When you have good, lifelong friends, betting with them or in most cases, against them, is a lifelong event. I have three very good and lifelong friends who I still bet with each and every year. And we don't have to shake hands to know the bet is on!

My three friends all live in Pennsylvania, where I grew up.

Bryan is a lifelong Pittsburgh Steelers fan. I've known Bryan longer than anyone in my life, other than family members. As five year olds, I remember my mother calling his to find out where he lived and if it was OK for me to walk to his house and play. He lived around the corner. We did play that day. Silly putty on his living room floor. I can still remember pressing the putty against the funny papers and pulling up the putty to see the faces of the characters.

Amazing what the mind keeps and how sometimes, someone reminds you of a moment and you have no recollection at all. Anyway, it was a long time ago, but started a lifelong friendship.

Bryan became a Steelers fan through his family, mostly his Dad, who relocated to Eastern Pennsylvania to work in the steel mill when the economy and mostly steel production was booming. I guess that was in the 60's or early 70's. His family brought their love for Pittsburgh sports across the Keystone State and another Steelers fan was born.

Another lifelong friend is Tom, a Raiders fan.

Tom's grandparents were Bryan's neighbors so he was often in the neighborhood as we were growing up. I'm sure he's told me once or twice how he became a Raiders fan, I believe through an Aunt of his, but I can't remember the entire story in detail. Not that it matters. For as long as I've known Tom, he's bled Silver and Black.

As young kids, I can remember standing with Tom and Bryan under the light pole in front of Bryan's house, in cold temperatures, arguing whose team was the greatest of them all. Bryan usually started and ended the argument with one gesture from his hand. No, he didn't give us the finger. He held up four fingers, as if to say, "The Steelers have four rings...therefore, this discussion is over!"

But that didn't necessarily stop me or Tom from continuing the argument. At the time, the Cowboys had two rings. The Raiders also had two rings and had recently beaten the Eagles in the big game. So Tom would work with that. Arguing that his team just won and add to that, had beaten our hometown team.

I, on the other hand, would point out the Cowboys had two, but had made five, losing the other three by a TOTAL of 11 points! Unfortunately, two of those losses were to the Steelers, which didn't help my cause. Also, the Eagles beat the Cowboys in the conference championship game in order to play the Raiders in the big game, which also didn't help my efforts. But I argued anyway, citing my Cowboys had only two rings, but five big game MVP's! Even more than the Steelers who only had four.

This arguing would not only continue, but continues to this day. Only difference is, we've added another fan. A Viking's fan.

John came along somewhere in the 7th or 8th grade. For some reason, he just seemed to fit right in. I think it was because we all started going to Middle School, bringing us together from different elementary schools. Again, it just worked and therefore led to what we now affectionately call the Beer Bet.

Beer Bet is pretty much self-explanatory.

We'd bet and the winner gets beer. Not money. A case (24 bottles) of beer unless something else is requested by the winner.

Here's how it works.
Each season, without having to talk about it, we know our teams will either deliver us three cases of delicious beer or we're paying out one case. It has nothing to do with a team having a better record, although that does come into play. How could it not. But our bet is simply based on which team is actually still playing at a later date than any other team.

For example, if the Steelers make the playoffs but the Vikings, Raiders and Cowboys do not, then Bryan wins three cases of beer. Simply because the Steelers were still playing once the playoffs began. This has happened from time to time with only one team making the playoffs and makes for an easy fridge filling victory for the winner!

The best seasons are when all the teams are good enough to make the playoffs, but that has been rare. As a matter of fact, I'm not sure, in all the years we've had this bet, that has actually happened. However, we have had years where the teams involved went head to head to see who would win all the marbles.

In the 2009 season, the Vikings hosted the Cowboys in a divisional playoff game. The Vikings destroyed the Cowboys and I, along with Bryan and Tom owed John a case of beer. I remember paying him the following weekend as we made our way to Wilmington, Delaware to do some LEGAL sports betting!

The best season for the beer bet, both personally and from a competitive standpoint, was when the Cowboys and Steelers played in the big game in the 90's. For the first and only time, it came down to the last game of the season. Bryan and I knew the winner would not only get plenty of beer but big time bragging rights. I needed the Cowboys to win to get revenge on those two Steelers wins in the 70's over the Cowboys. I did win, but so did Bryan, in a way.

When we first started the Beer Bet, the rules were a bit different. For about the first ten years or so, any team that made the playoffs won that fan a case of beer. In other words, if the Steelers, Vikings and Cowboys made the playoffs, the Raiders fan, in this case Tom would have to pay us each a case of beer. So instead of buying just one case, as the rules are today, the biggest loser, if you will, would have to buy THREE cases! This rule was changed, BECAUSE of Tom and his beloved yet often pathetic Raiders.

Year after year, it seemed Tom was paying a hefty price for his teams failures. The only season I can recall Tom actually winning beer was when the Silver and Black lost to Tampa Bay in the big game. Tough day for Tom and all Raiders fans that day, but at least he did get himself three cases. After a while, Tom, growing frustrated with the costs involved with our beer bet, asked for a rule change. He made it clear that ONLY the overall winner should get a case of beer and this way, each loser would only buy one case of beer each year. Bryan wasn't thrilled with the change...and why would he be? His Steelers almost always make the playoffs. But we gave into Tom's suggestion and that's how it stands today.

Now you may wonder why, with the three of them living in a Philadelphia suburb and me coming from a family of Eagles fans and marrying a woman whose family, for the most part, are Giants fans, never included a fan of either team in the Beer Bet. I mean, why not? If we are only paying one case each, what's the difference? We'll, we did have an Eagles fan in for a few years. Another friend of ours named Vinny. But, for whatever reason, it didn't work out. We dropped Vinny and it's just the four of us...again.

Perhaps forever. And that's just fine.

In Conclusion

I will leave you with a couple of points to chew on.

The professional football season should not start in early September. It should be changed to an 18 game regular season with opening day taking place in late September. This will allow the playoffs to continue through the month of February and the Super Bowl taking place in early March. Think about this, it's a sport fans dream come true! To have baseball playoffs into October and pro football just beginning. Then pro football running right into March Madness and Spring Training starts again! Sprinkle in a little hockey and pro basketball and you have quite a sports year without that incredibly difficult time I like to call the February/March withdrawals. I can't stand that time of year for sports. It's just the worst. Don't you agree?

Every year, that BIG GAME in February is something, isn't it? That being said, wouldn't it be nice if you could enjoy each week's games in the same fashion? You can. Not a regular season week goes by where, even if I'm alone, I'm not enjoying an exciting, down to the wire game. I honestly believe by setting a precedent with your significant other and the family members in your life and by taking advantage of this guide, you can increase your football viewing pleasure dramatically!

I wish you luck in this quest and was very happy I could help. I hope in the very least, this guide was entertaining for you the football fan, who just wants to sit back, relax and pop open some liquid refreshment.

Enjoy the games. Yes, all of the games! Have fun this Sunday!

I know I will.